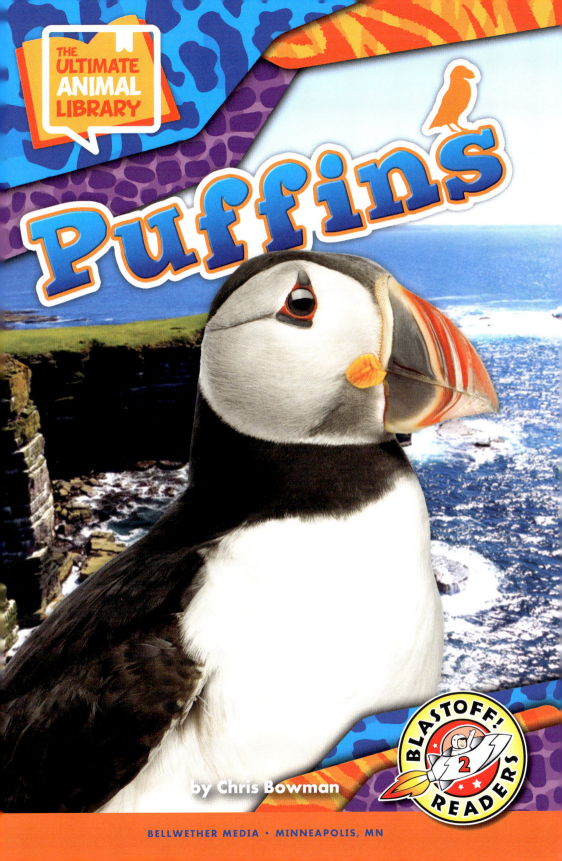

Blastoff! Readers are carefully developed by literacy experts to build reading stamina and move students toward fluency by combining standards-based content with developmentally appropriate text.

Level 1 provides the most support through repetition of high-frequency words, light text, predictable sentence patterns, and strong visual support.

Level 2 offers early readers a bit more challenge through varied sentences, increased text load, and text-supportive special features.

Level 3 advances early-fluent readers toward fluency through increased text load, less reliance on photos, advancing concepts, longer sentences, and more complex special features.

★ **Blastoff! Universe**

Reading Level

Grade K

Grades 1–3

Grade 4

This edition first published in 2026 by Bellwether Media, Inc.

No part of this publication may be reproduced in whole or in part without written permission of the publisher. For information regarding permission, write to Bellwether Media, Inc., Attention: Permissions Department, 3500 American Blvd W, Suite 150, Bloomington, MN 55431.

Library of Congress Cataloging-in-Publication Data

LC record for Puffins available at: https://lccn.loc.gov/2025003958

Text copyright © 2026 by Bellwether Media, Inc. BLASTOFF! READERS and associated logos are trademarks and/or registered trademarks of Bellwether Media, Inc. Bellwether Media is a division of FlutterBee Education Group.

Editor: Elizabeth Neuenfeldt   Series Designer: Veah Demmin

Printed in the United States of America, North Mankato, MN.

Table of Contents

What Are Puffins?	4
Deep Divers	12
Growing Up	18
Glossary	22
To Learn More	23
Index	24

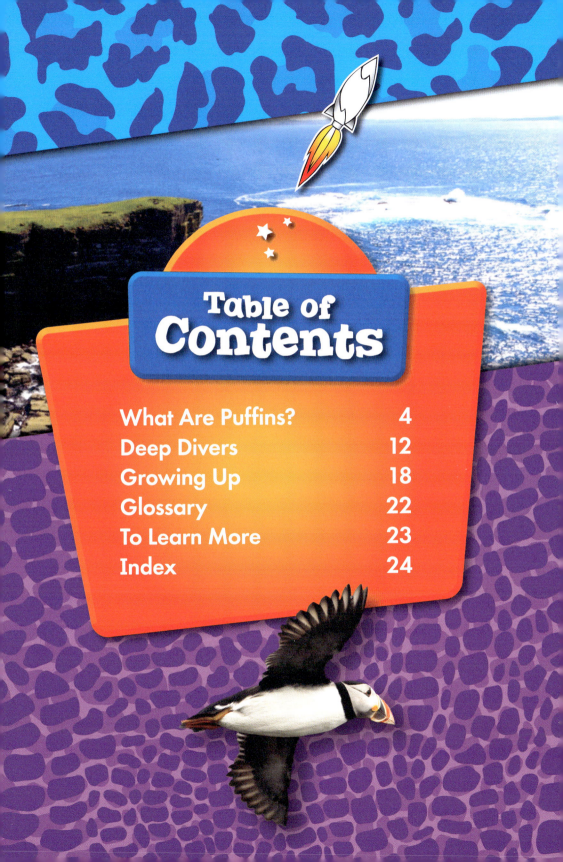

What Are Puffins?

Puffins are **marine** birds. They are named for their puffy shape. There are four puffin **species**. They live around the Atlantic and Pacific Oceans.

Puffins have small wings.
Their wings help them fly.

webbed feet

These birds also swim and dive. Their wings and **webbed feet** help them swim.

Puffins have dark feathers on their backs. Most have white bellies.

Most puffins have orange legs and feet.

Most puffins have big, colorful beaks. One species has yellow **tufts** behind their heads.

Puffins have white marks on their faces. Some have black marks by their eyes.

yellow tufts

Deep Divers

Puffins spend winter alone in open ocean waters. Some can dive up to 350 feet (107 meters) to find **prey**.

Their beaks can carry many fish at once.

In summer, puffins go to islands to nest and **mate**. They return to the same area each year.

They often find food in small groups.

burrow

Puffins build nests in **burrows** or between rocks. They often build nests near one another.

Nests keep them safe from **predators**.

Growing Up

A female puffin lays one egg each year. Both parents help keep the egg warm.

The egg **hatches** after about six weeks. A **puffling** comes out.

egg

puffling

The puffling stays in the nest for six weeks. Its parents bring it food to eat.

Then it goes to sea to find its own food!

Life of a Puffin

Name of Babies

 pufflings

Number of Eggs

 1

Time Spent with Parents

 about 6 weeks

Life Span

 around 40 years

Glossary

burrows—tunnels or holes in the ground used as animals' homes

hatches—breaks open

marine—related to the sea

mate—to come together to make young

predators—animals that hunt other animals for food

prey—animals that are hunted by other animals for food

puffling—a baby puffin

species—kinds of an animal

tufts—bunches of feathers

webbed feet—feet with skin that connects the toes

To Learn More

AT THE LIBRARY

Kenney, Karen Latchana. *Macaws*. Minneapolis, Minn.: Bellwether Media, 2021.

Rathburn, Betsy. *Brilliant Birds*. Minneapolis, Minn.: Bellwether Media, 2023.

Sabelko, Rebecca. *Penguin*. Minneapolis, Minn.: Bellwether Media, 2021.

ON THE WEB

FACTSURFER

Factsurfer.com gives you a safe, fun way to find more information.

1. Go to www.factsurfer.com.

2. Enter "puffins" into the search box and click 🔍.

3. Select your book cover to see a list of related content.

Index

Atlantic Ocean, 4
backs, 8
beaks, 10, 11, 13
bellies, 8
birds, 4, 7
colors, 8, 9, 10
dive, 7, 12
egg, 18
feathers, 8
feet, 9
females, 18
fly, 6
food, 13, 15, 17, 20, 21
groups, 15
islands, 14
legs, 9
life of a puffin, 21
marks, 10
mate, 14
name, 4
nest, 14, 16, 17, 20

Pacific Ocean, 4
parents, 18, 20
predators, 17
prey, 12
puffling, 18, 19, 20
range, 4, 5
size, 6, 10
species, 4, 10
spot a puffin, 11
status, 5
summer, 14
swim, 7
tufts, 10
waters, 12
webbed feet, 6, 7
wings, 6, 7
winter, 12

The images in this book are reproduced through the courtesy of: Eric Isselee, cover (puffin); Dr. Stefan Matthies, cover background, interior background; AnnstasAg, cover (puffin icon); birdiegal, p. 3; shaitan1985, p. 4; PictishImages, p. 6; whitcomberd, p. 7; markmedcalf, p. 8; Inichetti, p. 9; Nick Taurus, p. 10; MarekLuthardt, pp. 10-11; Eric Isselée, pp. 11, 23; Wirestock, p. 12; Martin, p. 13; Fotorequest, p. 14; G.Gambacciani, p. 15; 13threephotography, pp. 16-17; vaclav, p. 17 (polar bears); Paul, p. 17 (fish); JAG IMAGES, p. 17 (black-backed gulls); Jo, p. 17 (puffin); Arthur van der Kooj, p. 17 (foxes); Maximilian cabinet, p. 18; MulanPhoto, pp. 18-19; KODAKovic, p. 20; Luis, p. 21.